GOOD HEALTH
& LONG LIFE

Another Perspective

Rich Kanyali

Good Health and Long Life: Another Perspective

ISBN: 978-1-64204-420-1

Author of *Jesus; God or Man?*

Published by:

Rich Kanyali Ministries
P.O Box 243
Woodland Park Co 80866

RichKanyaliministries.com

info@richkanyaliministries.com

Table of Contents

Introduction

Over a long period of time, I have carefully observed how much good health is necessary for a long life. However, I have a few concerns about good health being the main or only factor necessary for living a long life.

I have seen people tie long life to good health and exercise alone. Although I do not disagree that these things play a part in someone's good health and longevity, they have been blown way out of proportion. There is no longer any balance, and people have come to think that all they need to do to live is just be healthy, take vitamin pills, eat well, go to gym, and on and on the list goes.

Unfortunately, too much emphasis has been put on the physical things, neglecting that a spiritual and soulish part of us has to be acknowledged as well.

When we look at magazines, Christian bookstores, news, and commercials, it's like everyone is advertising weight loss—get skinny, exercise, get weight-loss surgery, and so forth. I tend to wonder why people neglect the spiritual part of their health, which I believe is more important than the physical in this pursuit. I have concluded that many have not been taught or our teachers and spiritual leaders have not been as aggressive teaching the spiritual side of health as the world is on the physical aspects of good health.

But the very ignored truth is that your spiritual health is more important than your physical health. Unfortunately, many people don't know this; but even more, many don't even believe this. We have placed a cat before a horse!

Have you read James 2:26? It says that a body without the spirit is dead. Once there is no spirit, the body is just useless. It's got to be buried. It's dead. Genesis 2:7 says that God created man out of the ground, but man was not alive until God breathed in him the breath of life, which I believe was the spirit. God's breath gave us life. He blew His Spirit into us and created our human spirit. The spirit is what gives life (2 Cor. 3:6).

Man is not just a physical body. Man is spirit, soul, and body. It is wrong to only focus on the body (physical) and ignore the spirit and soul realms, which are also significant, if not more so. My intention is not to talk about your spirit, soul, and body, but to establish a truth that you are a spirit. You are a spirit, with a soul, living in a body (1 Thess. 5:23).

I will be focusing on the spiritual and emotional part, since the whole world is focused on the physical, and I will show how important it is to your body and the part it plays in your longevity.

Furthermore, when a person wants to lose weight, all personal trainers, coaches, and doctors ask the same question: why are you looking to make this change? When losing weight, all specialists would agree that the desire has to diligently start from the inside out. It's not enough to just to want to lose weight, exercise, and eat healthy; a person must be willing and ready to make it a lifestyle change from within. The inside piece I am referring to is the spirit and soul that God has given you. For real change to take place, one must be spiritually healthy from the inside.

Let me ask, why is it that most medical practitioners always think that a certain pill will take care of people's problems? I say that not all of the problems people have are physical. You can't wake up someday and make a pill for every problem. Spiritual problems will need spiritual help. They have made stress pills, worry pills, and on the list flows.

I will be going through this "pill" that I have discovered that can heal the spiritual, soulish (emotional), and physical problems.

Just as you put faith in all other pills to take care of your problems, you need to put faith in this pill to get the benefit that supersedes all other pills. This pill is the "Gos-pill"—the Gospel. The good news of God's Word is the best kind of pill, one that will give you the best stability you can ever get.

Chapter One

Good Health As Your Soul Prospers

Beloved, I wish above all things that thou mayest prosper and be in health, even as thy soul prospereth.
— 3 John 1:2

God desires you to be in good health. He wants your physical body to be healthy just as He desires your spiritual and soulish realms to be healthy.

However, God desires you to understand that Spiritual health is way better than the physical. Having spiritual health could produce health in your physical body to the degree you let it. The major problem is that people today talk about all these physical things, but don't acknowledge the spiritual part at all. Yet, it's just as important if not more so. So people die healthy and go to hell. Of what benefit is that? Why would someone live their whole life caring about the less relevant (physical) while ignoring the most relevant (spiritual)?

What does it profit a man if he shall gain the whole health (physical) and lose his or her soul in hell? The answer is NOTHING. Yes, nothing.

Today, we live in a world of misplaced priorities. People focus on the less relevant and ignore the most relevant. I am not against physical health. As a matter of fact, I am just promoting it by offering and focusing on the biblical and godly view of health. The truth is we can't just ignore what God's Word says and only focus on what the doctors, nutritionists, and dietitians say. What God has to say should stand taller than what anyone else has to say. Period. We have to ask, what does God say about it? God's opinion is better than the whole world's opinion on health or anything else. I prefer and recommend the principles and lessons the Bible teaches to help us maintain a good health and long life.

What Promotes Good Health?

I strongly believe that if we put scripture ahead of the physical, we would be healthier accidentally than we ever would have been on purpose by putting the physical ahead.

I tell you, I know of a very powerful man of God who has over thirtyeight years of supernatural health and he will tell you that it's not because of food or exercise, but godliness.

Food and exercise are not as important as most people have made them appear.

I can't prove this, but I believe about 19 percent of your health comes from the food you eat and exercise. Most people would argue that these things are more than 91 percent. I believe that living a godly life, honoring parents, departing from evil (sin), keeping our minds stayed on the Lord and His Word, rejoicing in the Lord and His Word and so forth are more important than these natural things.

We should not be too humanistic, ignoring spiritual roots to things and only trying to find a physical, organic reason for everything. For instance, people say, "You are depressed due to lack of certain chemicals." Yet the reason you lack certain chemicals is because you're depressed. God's Word has a solution to this problem — Rejoice in the Lord and encourage yourself in Him. Or, you can take a pill and have someone dope you up so you can function. That's not the right way to do it.

Many people today are promoting all kinds of natural health products. They are encouraging you to go on a vegetarian diet, eat barley grain, and so forth. For Christians to have more emphasis on diet and exercise than teaching the Word is comparable to putting all your resources in the less significant and neglecting the most significant. Now I am not saying these things are not important, but I don't believe that the way you exercise or what you eat determines 90 or 99% of your health. The Bible doesn't teach that.

I have heard that clinical studies have shown that godliness positively affects health. Prayer has been proven by researchers to speed recovery.

The gospel is the power of God unto salvation (forgiveness of sins, healing, health, prosperity and deliverance). The good news of God's love toward you will produce a supernatural healing and health in your body. Just knowing how much God loves you would break depression from your life. It will change your thinking and reaction, producing healing.

Godliness

For bodily exercise profiteth little: but godliness is profitable unto all things, having promise of the life that now is, and of that which is to come.

— 1 Timothy 4:8

Godliness profits in all things. That's what the scripture teaches us. ALL things! Not in just one thing—physical, but all things (Spiritual, soulish and physical). The Word is profitable to the physical, soulish, and spiritual realm. There is nothing else like that. Nothing compares to godliness. There is nothing you can do physically that can profit you in both the physical, soulish and spiritual as GODLINESS.

It's good and important to exercise, but godliness is much more profitable. It has a promise in this life — long life (Proverbs 10:27) — and in the life to come. What's better? But why are people neglecting this great deal. With godliness you shoot three birds with one stone.

Have you considered receiving Jesus in your life? It's crucial that you know you have promises in this life and in the life to come.

Righteousness = Life

As righteousness tendeth to life: so he that pursueth evil pursueth it to his own death.

— Proverbs 11:19

The above scripture teaches clearly that righteousness tends to life. The Amplified version uses the word "attains." We all agree that we need a good health to live, however few of us understand that it is really impossible to have good health without righteousness. Having a personal relationship with Jesus is the biggest step towards the direction of good health and a long life. We have to be in right standing with God, which comes by faith in Jesus as our Lord and Savior. By so doing, we receive a change in heart which literally enables us and helps us to live a godly and righteous life.

If we pursue or go after evil, we are digging our own grave. We are running after death. We will be destroyed sooner or later. This is a tremendous piece of wisdom that many have bypassed. It's so simple. You will need someone's help to misunderstand it.

Chapter Two

Taking Heed To God's Word

Wherewithal shall a young man cleanse his way? by taking heed thereto according to thy word. Thy word have I hid in mine heart, that I might not sin against thee.
— Psalms 119:9, 11

One of the other ways to be healthy is taking heed to God's Word and not only heeding to the word of your doctor or professor. You can make your ways prosperous and healthy by learning from God and following His wisdom and instructions.

God being the one that created you has much to say about your body and how to keep it healthy more than anyone else. Medical practitioners also have bodies like you and me.

He sent his word, and healed them, and delivered them from their destructions.
— Psalms 107:20

Just in case you get sick, God's Word is meant to be your daily prescription. It will heal your body better than any pill, and the good news is that with it there are no side effects. It's better. Proverbs 4:20-12 says that if you incline your ear to God's Word, it will be life unto those that find and heed to it and also health to all their flesh.

Now I don't believe anyone can have total health without taking heed to God's Word or the principles from God's Word whether they know them or not. People may look healthy to a certain degree, but the Bible says that health to <u>all their flesh</u> comes from God's Word. There is no other way. Spiritual health principles from God's Word thrive above physical principles. Now, you may say, "Oh, but I do not read the Bible, how can I get so healthy like that?" Well, there is no shortcut. You have to start reading and believing God's Word. It is to your benefit. It's rich in knowledge and wisdom. I challenge you to consider God's Word (The Holy Bible). It will be health to your spirit, soul, and body.

So, what does the Word say?

Life To All Their Flesh

For they are life unto those that find them, and health to all their flesh.

— Proverbs 4:22

This scripture says that God's Word is life to those that find it. God's Word is not life to everyone, but to those who find it. This clearly shows that there has to be some sort of seeking. We have to seek and pursue it. It won't happen naturally or automatically. There has got to be some effort on our part.

This passage of scripture also reveals that God's Word is not just health to their flesh, but to all their flesh. Nothing out there is health to all your flesh. Only God's Word meets this standard. Why would someone seek to be healthy and yet ignore this powerful passage of scripture?

I believe this scripture, as well as many others, explains why most people who are godly are healthier. They keep God's Word and it is health to **all** their flesh.

Thinking

For as he thinketh in his heart, so is he: Eat and drink, saith he to thee; but his heart is not with thee.

— Proverbs 23:7

Many of the physical problems people have are directly proportional to how they have been thinking or how they are thinking. You will be a product of your thoughts, and you are a product of your thoughts.

Your life will go in the direction of your dominant thoughts. If you think negatively, you will get negative results. If you think sick, you will be. If you think defeat, you will be, and so on.

This truth from the Bible will get your emotions under control just through thinking right, and I have to say that you don't need a pill to get these results. All you need is God's Word; e.g. Proverbs 23:7. And as you put faith in this and apply it to your life; it will work more than any pill.

Finally, brethren, whatsoever things are true, whatsoever things are honest, whatsoever things are just, whatsoever things are pure, whatsoever things are lovely, whatsoever things are of good report; if there be any virtue, and if there be any praise, think on these things. Those things, which ye have both learned, and received, and heard, and seen in me, do: and the God of peace shall be with you.

— Philippians 4:8-9

This passage of Scripture says that we must think on the right things: things that are true, honest (having or showing qualities of high moral character), just (equitable — in character or act — by implication, innocent, holy), pure (clean, i.e. figuratively, innocent, modest, perfect), lovely, of good report, with virtue, and praiseworthy. This is totally in our control. We choose what we think upon. There is nothing like, "I just can't help it." Yes, you can. We have to control our thinking in order to control our emotional stability. These two are intertwined. This will release life to our physical bodies, hence producing good health and life.

A Merry Heart

A merry heart doeth good like a medicine: but a broken spirit drieth the bones.

— Proverbs 17:22

Operating in joy will do you good like a medicine. This isn't saying that you have to take a happy pill to be joyful. Just operate in joy and you will be all right. For example, if you understood how much God loves you, you would be joyful regardless of your problems. You would be rejoicing. It's an antidote to depression and stress.

Now you may say that you have tried it and it didn't work. If you are just trying it, it may never work. You have to do it. Just do it.

I can't tell you how many times medicinal pills and drugs have not worked. People have died taking pills. They don't always work. Now, don't get me wrong; nothing is wrong with taking pills or medicine if you aren't believing God. Go right ahead. I am not against doctors or medicine; if it were not for doctors and medical practitioners, many Christians would have been dead by now because they weren't believing God for their healing.

Now, you may say, "Oh, I can still take my pill while trusting God to heal me, right?" Well, you may choose to do it that way as long as you don't die. God will meet you where your faith is. I strongly believe that doctors and God are all on the same side. Both are out to heal and cure the sick. Healing the sick and curing diseases is not the work of the devil. What you believe in your heart is what you will receive not what someone else believes in their heart. The way God led someone else is not necessarily the way He will lead you. Seek God and follow His instructions for you. God and medical science are working together for the same end result—to restore health to the sick and preserve lives. It doesn't violate our faith for healing, to go to the doctor if that is where our faith is. We shouldn't condemn others for talking steps of faith that are real to them at that time.

Doctors and God are not opposing each other. **The best doctrine is living. We are more useful to God alive than dead!** God will always meet people where they are not where we are. We should encourage people in their faith not our faith. People should act on what they have faith for.

I am not against pills and medicine, but research has shown the terrible side effects of pills, medicine, and drugs. I have discovered that, sometimes, you would rather be sick than to take medicine or certain drugs.

The side effects of drugs (medicine) are sometimes worse than the disease itself. Many people have died quicker through taking medicine than the disease would have killed them. They would have lived longer without going to see the doctor who later prescribed drugs that broke down their immune system.

Going back to my point, the way we think is important; and operating in joy is good for your health. You don't have to eat healthy or live in the gym to fix this emotional problem.

I read an article that said most people's diseases are connected to their emotions or emotional instability. So let me ask a question, how do you then heal such diseases? Do you advocate eating well, losing weight, etc.? No, you have to deal with the root. God's Word has the answer to that. It's unique and it's the word of the Chief Architect of our physical bodies. It tells you what to do. For example, it teaches you how to think right and control your thinking and how to be joyful and rejoice evermore.

Peace

For to be carnally minded is death; but to be spiritually minded is life and peace.

— Romans 8:6

Peace is an a state of tranquility that a drug cannot purchase. You cannot just lay your hand on another and command peace to flow. Peace flows from the inside out. It is not based on the circumstances around you. Unlike happiness, you can be peaceful in the midst of turmoil, tragedy and problems.

God's word shows us how to get peace.

Romans 8:6 says that peace is a result of being spiritually minded. To be spiritually minded is to have our **mind set** on the things of the Spirit, the things of God. It is to think, dominate, and focus your attention on God's Word and promises and when you do so, the result is God's kind of peace circulating your soul.

Being spiritually minded doesn't tend to life; it is life and peace. Mathematically, you would say that spiritual mindedness = life + peace.

If you say that you are spiritually minded but aren't getting these results, then you are doing something wrong. You cannot focus on the news and all these negative reports from all over and expect to be peaceful. You have to be dominated by what God says — not anyone else! — and then will you have life and peace flow within you.

Peace is essential to your physical health.

Thou wilt keep him in perfect peace, whose mind is stayed on thee: because he trusteth in thee.

— Isaiah 26:3

This scripture complements and adds ingredients to Romans 8:6. It says that God will keep you in perfect peace if your mind is stayed on Him.

Now, if you didn't know, God will keep you in perfect peace through His Word. It's His Word that has the promises and words of peace; and it's through it you will be able to keep your mind single-focused on Him.

Prayer

For every creature of God is good, and nothing to be refused, if it be received with thanksgiving: For it is sanctified by the word of God and prayer.

— 1 Timothy 4:4-5

The Bible says that food is sanctified (cleansed) by the Word of God and prayer.

Praying over your food is essential to your health. These are things that are not taught by the dietitians, nutritionists, and gym instructors. All they are concerned about is the physical, ignoring tremendous effects from the spiritual. Prayer cleanses your food. God's Word, spoken over what you eat, could save your health—big time! It could literally kill pending germs instantly. Yes, it would and it does.

"Oh no, I don't believe that stuff," you may say. Well, then it won't work for you. If you don't believe it, it's not going to work for you. "Why is that?" you may think. It's because you don't believe it. It only works for those that believe it.

Chapter Three

The Thief

The thief cometh not, but for to steal, and to kill, and to destroy: I am come that they might have life, and that they might have it more abundantly.

— John 10:10

Satan is a thief, a killer, and a destroyer. Satan cuts people's lives short. He kills them. But he doesn't kill whoever he finds. He devours those who submit to him and do not resist him (1 Peter 5:8). One of the ways people submit to Satan is through **ungodly living**. Now, although God loves you, you cannot just open the door to Satan to come in to destroy and cut your life short. Today we see a lot of young men and women killed as a result of choosing to live ungodly lives. No one takes responsibility anymore, but instead we blame God for these tragedies. If we only knew John 10:10, we would not blame God because we would know He isn't the author of death. It's not God that started death. He never created it. He created life and we created death. Death was never begun by God.

By living a godly life we close a door to Satan (the killer) so he doesn't come in and cut our lives short.

Evil Slays

Evil shall slay the wicked: and they that hate the righteous shall be desolate.

— Psalms 34:21

The above verse clearly teaches that evil shall kill the ungodly (the wicked). Living an ungodly life will destroy and kill the godly and ungodly. So, for you to live long, you have to factor in the above scripture. You can't just live like the devil and expect to live long. Your life will be cut short. You won't enjoy the blessing of long life.

It's very simple; if you want to live longer quit being wicked.

Departing From Evil

Depart from evil, and do good; and dwell for evermore.

— Psalms 37:27

This verse says that for you to dwell evermore, you have to depart from evil and do good. Departing from evil is impossible without doing good. This scripture is stressing furthermore that departing from evil will get you to dwell evermore, which is to say to live longer.

Most people can't see a connection between departing from sin (evil) and their health. They think they can live anyway they want (indulge all their ungodly desires) and at the same time have a bolstering good physical health. I disagree. I believe there is an immense connection between the two.

Many individuals advocate eating well and going to gym, but they neglect the truth that living a sinful life is one of the main inroads to physical problems in people's lives. I think you can't separate the two if you want good health results.

Jesus died for the sins of the whole world and, just to remind you, your sins (past, present and future) have been paid for in full by the Lord Jesus Christ. So, before God, sin is no longer an issue to our relationship with Him. The war is over between God and the sins of mankind. Actually, people will go to hell with their sins already paid for having rejected the payment made by the Lord Jesus Christ for their sins, and they will have to pay for them in hell for all eternity. It's simple: receive Jesus in your life as your personal Lord and Savior and believe that He died and rose again from the dead for you so that payment for your sins will be imputed to your account. This is the most important decision you will ever make. God loves you whether you sin or not and His love for you is not based on your actions, works, or performance. It's unconditional.

So, sin is not a big deal anymore vertically(between you and God), but horizontally (between you and other people) sin or evil will open a door for problems — physical and emotional — in your life.

> *Know ye not, that to whom ye yield yourselves servants to obey, his servants ye are to whom ye obey; whether of sin unto death or of obedience unto righteousness?*
>
> — Romans 6:16

The truth is that failure to depart from evil will get your body in huge physical health problems which good diet and exercise cannot get rid of. Satan will put diseases and sickness in your body. You will get sick and you might cut your life short through eventual disease and sickness. You must quit!

Quitting has nothing to do with God's love for you or not. He loves you whether you quit or not. For instance, sexual perversion will open your body to emotional problems, AIDS, anal diseases, cancers, and on the list goes. For almost every STD I have looked up, it is extremely higher in homosexuals than in the heterosexuals. This is one example of how an ungodly lifestyle opens you up to a chain of sicknesses and diseases which will destroy your life. You can't live long living like the devil.

> What man is he that desireth life, and loveth many days, that he may see good? Keep thy tongue from evil, and thy lips from speaking guile. Depart from evil, and do good; seek peace, and pursue it.
> — Psalms 34:12-14

The Bible has a lot to say about departing from evil, but interestingly enough it adds benefits to it such as long life, good health, etc.

You can't continue living like the devil and expect good health and long life to be a reality. You must depart from evil.

If you want life and want to see good, you have to depart from evil and do good. Seek peace and pursue it. There is no way around it. You have to depart from sin and evil, quit living in sin and acting like the devil.

Sin is like feces. It attracts flies which spread diseases. So, if you allow your body to be an abode for sin like a toilet or pit latrine, you will harbor and accommodate all sorts of diseases.

People who live like the devil have a lot of physical and emotional problems to deal with which is an impediment to long life and good health.

Romans 6:16 says that if you yield your body to sin, you become a servant of that sin and it's author—Satan.

Satan is a thief. The Bible says he comes to steal, kill, and destroy. One of the ways he does that is through sickness and diseases that come through living in sin.

> *He that loveth pleasure shall be a poor man: he that loveth wine and oil shall not be rich.*
>
> — Proverbs 21:17

Another thing is that most people wonder why they are broke (Proverbs 21:17; 23:21). They don't realize that not departing from evil is expensive. Living a life of sin is very costly. It will rob you of your wealth and health. You will get sick and spend your money at the doctor. It's better to be healthy than to have thousands of dollars to see a doctor. The Bible says that the way of the transgressor is hard (Proverbs 13:15). Living in sin is hard. You literally have to do the hard thing to live in sin. You have to work so hard to live in sin. It's not easy; it's really hard. Sometimes I wonder why people love doing the hard thing.

Anyway, what I am trying to say is that sin is not good for you. Just as people emphasize eating healthy and exercising, I am emphasizing that departing from evil is a greater healthy initiative.

I am not trying to condemn anyone. Like I said earlier on, Jesus loves you regardless of your folly. God loves you, but it's stupid to ruin your life. I am saying all these things because I love you and I want you to reap the benefits of living a holy life. That's why I say that it is of great significance to depart from evil in order to live a healthy and a long life.

I know of a guy who lives from paycheck to paycheck because of his smoking habits. He is ever broke! Yet, at the same time he is destroying his life willfully with his own money. He works so, so hard to destroy his life! Unfortunately, many people are doing this.

In Jesus is the power to set such a person free if they want to be and are also willing to cooperate.

Chapter Four

The Merciful Man

The merciful man doeth good to his own soul: but he that is cruel troubleth his own flesh.

— Proverbs 11:17

The merciful and generous man benefits his soul [for his behavior returns to bless him], But the cruel and callous man does himself harm.

— Proverbs 11:17 (Amplified)

When you're kind to others, you help yourself; when you're cruel to others, you hurt yourself.

— Proverbs 11:17 (The Message)

Being cruel (violent, causing, suffering and pain) is very dangerous; not just to the people we try to hurt, but to us. We are doing damage to ourselves when we are not merciful. If we continue in that direction, we are going to cut our lives short. It's not just adultery, sexual perversion, smoking and drinking that will hurt us, but being cruel is equally dangerous. If we are merciful, we are preserving our life but if we are out to cause others to suffer, we are saying good bye to our own life. We will surely reap what we sow.

Honoring Parents

Honour thy father and thy mother: that thy days may be long upon the land which the LORD thy God giveth thee.

— Exodus 20:12

Honoring your parents means to give due respect, to esteem, to obey, and to care for. The Bible admonishes us to honor our parents, which in return will give us long days upon the earth. This verse teaches us that failure to honor, respect, and esteem your father and mother could rob us of the blessing of living longer.

Today, people only focus on physical things and neglect the fact that respecting, esteeming, and taking care of our parents is a very necessary ingredient for us to live longer. People who don't honor their fathers and mothers don't live long. Many are sickly and feeble, which later cuts their lives short. We have to purposefully do what it takes to honor our parents. Now, you might be thinking of a few people you know that have lived long yet they have been very dishonoring to their parents in your estimate and there are others you know that have honored their parents but they are long gone. Here is what I have to say about this, it's not either or but a combination of all what we have talked about. You can't choose honoring your parents and still live an ungodly lifestyle. We have to set our hearts to living a godly lifestyle.

I once heard of a research study, unfortunately I can't recall from where. But this research said that the Japanese and Chinese live longer than most people on the earth. The research went on to say that they discovered that one of the reasons is because they eat more fish and generally have a healthier diet.

I really disagree. I don't believe that is the reason. I believe they are missing out on something far greater than eating fish. Why is it that people just try to attach and relate everything to something physical? Is there not any another explanation that isn't only physical? Why isn't there any research that points to something else than the physical?

You may say, "Oh, the Japanese and the Chinese don't eat too much. See, they use very small plates, eat less milk, butter, and dairy. They drink tea, eat fish, and lots of soy."

But is this all that it takes to live long? I believe that the answer to why they live long is found in Exodus 20:12. The Japanese and the Chinese honor their parents more than anyone I know. They also go to the extreme of worshiping their parents and ancestors, which I truly believe is wrong but my point is that they honor their parents. They practice Exodus 20:12 whether they know it or not, and it yields the fruit of long life.

You have to start honoring and loving your father and mother. Eating well and exercising will not cut the edge nor will it be a substitute for honoring our parents. It takes a combination of the two, but much more the spiritual aspect which in this instance is honoring our parents. If you want to live long you have to adapt this godly principle.

The Dangers of Envy

A sound heart is the life of the flesh: but envy the rottenness of the bones.

— Proverbs 14:30

As I continue to encourage you to quit evil, envy is another barrier to health that people overlook yet ought to quit. It is rottenness to the bones. Envy opens doors to rottenness— sickness. It's like a cancer. Envy invites sickness and diseases in your body. The way to be biblically healthy is to quit evil, including envy.

James 3:16 says that "For where envying and strife is, there is confusion and every evil work." Envy and strife are worse than anything you could imagine. They open up a door to **EVERY** evil work such as demonic activity, loss, sickness, poverty, depression, death, destruction, misery, sufferings, pain, divorce, perversion, you name it.

Many people living in envy, jealousy, and hatred are sick physically which is most possibly the cause of whichever disease they might be suffering from. The root is in envy, jealousy and hatred as the bible says. If you want to be completely healthy, you must depart from evil.

Gluttony

Gluttony is a sin. If we want to be healthy, we have to quit being gluttons. "Oh, I can't give up my junk food just so that I can be healthy. I want to eat what I want when I want and as much of it as I want." Well that's the problem. You can't just eat as an animal and expect to keep the weight of a healthy human being. Put your fork down. Drop it!

Although people out there that teach being healthy have not told you, the concept of not overeating is not just physical. It is first a spiritual principle. They have taken that concept from the Bible although they never say so nor give credit to God for His wisdom and brilliance. Anyone alive in our society knows well how true this is. Overeating (gluttony) is not good for you and will play a major part in hampering your good health.

Many surveys reveal that the more food you eat, the more you are bound to gain excessive weight. Eating too much will reward you with too much weight. Although I am not against fat folks, this I will tell you: most of them love food and eat too much of it when they aren't even hungry. Eating is a necessity and a hobby to some of them. Too much weight is usually linked to over eating, too many calories, and too much fatty foods. If eating too much is a cause of health problems, it's crucial to remember that the Bible teaches against over eating. And, taking heed would save you a lot of problems.

Now, I am not saying that you should starve yourself. Of course not! Today we live in a model-built world where skinny is good, but starving yourself to get skinny is bad. Whether you are fat or skinny, you are not better than anyone else. God loves all of these people regardless of their size and weight, but He also teaches you to be healthy through His Word. Departing from gluttony would do you some good in regards to your health and long life. You don't have to drink drinks that cut your appetite or take pills to do the same. Just quit over eating.

Keep Thy WEIGHT With All Diligence?

Keep thy heart with all diligence; for out of it are the issues of life.

— Proverbs 4:23

Today, we live as if our weight is the most important thing. We protect it, and will do anything to lose a pound and not gain a pound. Unfortunately, this is not the same effort directed towards keeping our hearts as the above scripture tells us to do. This verse does not tell us to keep our weight with all diligence.

There is nothing that we are admonished to keep with all diligence like our hearts, mainly because out of our hearts flows the issues (springs and sources) of life. This is saying that our heart is more important than anything else. This passage of scripture is placing a greater priority on our heart (Spirit and soul), not our weight. I am not saying that our physical health is not important, but I am saying that our spiritual heart is much more important and needs the greatest attention, not your weight.

Vain Labor

Except the LORD build the house, they labour in

vain that build it: except the LORD keep the city, the watchmen waketh but in vain.

— Psalms 127:1

Doing anything without God being in it is a big waste. Building a house, building good health and long life, or building a healthy marriage, is a waste of time without factoring in God and His biblical principles. Leaning on your own understanding will only get you so far.

If you can achieve your goals without trusting in God, you need to rewrite your goals. If you can succeed without dependence on God, you have not succeeded. True success in God's eyes depends on whether we trusted Him or not. It doesn't depend on our end result—Success.

Here is my point; we can't trust God in just a few things. We must trust Him in everything, even our health and long life; otherwise we won't arrive where God wants us to be. I defy longevity without these biblical godly principles.

God plays a big role in any success you would love to achieve, including a long life and good health. That's why the above scripture says that except the Lord build the house; they which labor do so but in vain. In other words, they are working for nothing because God is not in it. They are wasting time, resources and energy. It's true, you better believe it.

And except the Lord keeps the city, they that keep it do so but in vain. God is the Supreme Watchman that neither sleeps nor slumbers, and we can't just leave Him out of the equation to get our desired results. I hope this encourages you to get God and His principles involved in everything you do.

A doctor may have told you that it's over, but a doctor should not have the final word in your life. God should. Over the years, I have learned not to take the word of man (physicians) as final, but only the Word of God. God has proven more trustworthy and accurate than any man. You may refuse the doctor's report and take what the Bible says and you will live beyond what the doctor has said.

Chapter Five

Satisfaction of Long Life

With long life I will satisfy him, and shew him my salvation.

— Psalms 91:16

It is evident and intuitive that people want to live long. Although there will be some that say or act like they don't want to, it's a yearning desire that is true in the vast majority of mankind. This is why there is ongoing research to heal "incurable diseases."

This desire to live long and healthy is furthermore explained by the way people are carefully considering what they eat and the way they are exercising. They do so to position themselves to allow their bodies to give them an extra edge to live longer.

I have discussed how it is greatly important to focus on the biblical way to be healthy than the physical way. I have shown that it is important to know that the spiritual aspect of our lives plays a greater and better role to our health, believe it or not.

Just as good health is a blessing from God, so is long life. Long life doesn't happen automatically, and there are biblical godly principles that you have to implement to see a long life besides just eating well and healthy, having good hygiene, and exercising.

I have shown that living an ungodly life will rob you of your health and longevity. I have also pointed out what the Bible has to say about long life in hope that you will open up your heart and receive these godly principles to help enhance your health and longevity.

God wants to satisfy you with long life if you are not satisfied. I guaranteed you this will happen through His Word.

I have heard stories of people who were given three weeks or so to live by the doctor and today they have lived over eight years beyond that. What made the difference was not the food they ate or the exercise they did, but by believing in God's Word. Their life was restored and spared. Godly principles from God's Word will take you this far, hence the need to focus on the spiritual more than the physical.

What man is he that desireth life, and loveth many days, that he may see good? Keep thy tongue from evil, and thy lips from speaking guile. Depart from evil, and do good; seek peace, and pursue it.

— Psalms 34:12

The verse above asks a question: "What man is he that desireth life, and loveth many days, that he may see good?"

Do you want to live long? Psalms 34:12-14 tells you what to do. But notice that it never talks about eating very healthy, exercising, and all these physical things people promote. No! It focuses solely on the spiritual part; not because the physical is not essential, but because the spiritual part is of greater importance and if implemented, it could fix the physical.

It tells you to keep your tongue (Proverbs 18:21) from evil and thy lips from speaking lies, to depart from evil, to do good, to seek peace and pursue it. You should not use your tongue in an immoral way which can cause harm to others, and you should quit living immoral lives. Instead, do good, and seek peace. By doing the above things, you will be playing a major role in your longevity. That's what God says. You will have many days.

Minimum Age

The days of our years are threescore years and ten; and if by reason of strength they be fourscore years, yet is their strength labour and sorrow; for it is soon cut off, and we fly away.

— Psalms 90:10

It is God's will for you to live long and that's why you have these scriptures proclaiming and teaching so. You don't have to accept dying young because according to God's Word (which expresses His will), the minimum is threescore and ten years (i.e. 3 x 20 = 60 +10 = 70 years of age). Notice that this is the minimum and not the maximum. I really believe that any death below the minimum is a premature death and it's not a part God's best for us. You may live to be more than seventy years old, but anything less is below the standard of God's will. It's long life, but not really long life, if you know what I mean.

God desires you to live long — at least seventy years. So, for you to get the minimum, you have to apply the godly principles that I am pointing out in this book so as to get there. Step up and shift into the highest gear. Don't be satisfied with anything less.

Length Of Days

My son, forget not my law; but let thine heart keep my commandments: For length of days, and long life, and peace, shall they add to thee.

— Proverbs 3:1-2

This scripture clearly states that hearkening to and keeping God's Word will help you to live longer and will prolong the length of thy days here on earth.

So, we should not ignore this spiritual truth, only focusing on the physical truths. I believe it's a grave mistake to ignore spiritual truth to only consider or facilitate the physical. There has to be a combination of the two to get tremendous results.

The fear of the LORD is the beginning of wisdom: and the knowledge of the holy is understanding. For by me thy days shall be multiplied, and the years of thy life shall be increased.

— Proverbs 9:10-11

The fear of the Lord, which is to depart from evil, will bring wisdom. Wisdom will multiply your days and increase the years of your life. Wisdom comes from God's Word which teaches us to fear the Lord and enables us to depart from evil.

Many people today are seeking to have their days multiplied and their years increased without considering this principle from God's Word.

I'm lamenting the ignorance exhibited in pursuit of good health and long life without the inclusion of God's Word. I think it's much more important to esteem God's Word to have a healthy life and longevity. I strongly believe that the number one way to promote good health and a long life is to teach people what God's Word has to say about it. This is what is mainly missing in all attempts to promote good health and a long life.

The Fear of the Lord

The fear of the LORD prolongeth days: but the years of the wicked shall be shortened.

— Proverbs 10:27

What if someone just eats healthy and does everything in the physical, yet he is wicked? Will he get the same results as this verse says? We can't just do everything right in the physical and yet be wicked and expect to live longer. This passage of scripture continues to hammer down the importance of the fear of the Lord and the benefit of prolonged and healthy life. Do you want to live long? You have to consider the fear of the Lord more than anything else.

What is the fear of the Lord? Proverbs 8:13 says that the fear of the Lord is to hate evil. Proverbs 16:6 says that by the fear of the Lord, men depart from evil. So, without hating evil or departing from it, there can't be the fear of the Lord. And the fear of the Lord comes from the Word of God, without which there are no prolonged days or life.

> *The fear of the LORD is a fountain of life, to depart from the snares of death.*
>
> — Proverbs 14:27

Since the fear of the Lord means to depart from evil, then this scripture can be read as, ***"Departing from evil** is a fountain of life, to depart from the snare of death."*

The word "fountain" used here means, a source, a spring or a wellspring of life. Departing from evil is a source, a spring and a wellspring of long life and will save you from falling into traps that may lead to death which cuts your life short.

> *The fear of the LORD tendeth to life: and he that hath it shall abide satisfied; he shall not be visited with evil.*
>
> — Proverbs 19:23

I know I already touched on what it means to fear the Lord, but this scripture goes on to further emphasize the importance of departing from evil and its result of longevity. Just in case you didn't get it the first, second, and third time, this scripture presents the same truth once again. It says that he that has this fear of the Lord shall abide satisfied. If we need or lack satisfaction, we need to fear the Lord—depart from evil. A long and healthy life flows and springs from the fear of the Lord.

Conclusion and Prayer for Healing

I challenge you to consider what the Word has to say about health and long life. My intent in writing this book is to get you to consider the other side (another perspective) of the coin that has been neglected. I hope and pray that you have learned a thing or two that you can apply in your life and enjoy a lengthy and healthy life here on earth.

Now, if you are sick or diseased, I want to take a moment and pray for you. I hate sickness and disease. This is one of the other reasons I have written this book. It's my heart and desire to see you walk in good health and long life. No one should accept disease and sickness, let alone to die young. If you can be agreement with me as I pray, you will and you can get healed. Some will get healed instantaneously, others in a few hours and others might take days and might be a lot more gradual but if you believe, you will and can get healed.

"Father I thank You for the healing that You purchased for the man or woman reading this

book. Thank You that it is your will to heal our bodies every time and every day. Thank You that You are an awesome, loving, and good God. Lord, right now I release Your healing power to flow into the body of the reader to cause healing to happen. It doesn't matter what the doctor has said or what their report is, we choose to believe Your report and command healing into this physical body in the name of Jesus. This man or woman shall live and not die (Psalm 118:17). Today the reader of this book will see Your power, glory and salvation manifest in his or her life. Now, you pain, you sickness, you disease (I'm speaking to you cancer — at any stage — or brain disease, or AIDS) and you filthy spirit of infirmity and oppression… I curse you, I rebuke you, and I command you to GET out of the reader's body in Jesus' Name. I speak and command you viruses, bacteria, and germs to die right now. I nullify every negative report and I bless and declare this reader healed and well in Jesus' Name. I speak and decree a supernatural restoration of those parts of your body that have been affected by any disease and sickness. Be healed and restored in Jesus' Name. Amen! Hallelujah. Thank you, Jesus.

Now, begin to do what you couldn't do. Get up, stretch, move your hands, move your legs. Do something you couldn't do. YOU ARE HEALED! Some of you have gotten healed right now and some of you it might take a minute, an hour, or a day, but don't leave this default position that you have been healed. God's power has defeated whatever was afflicting you. Hallelujah! Thank You, Jesus.

Receive Jesus As Your Savior

Deciding to receive Jesus Christ as your Lord and Savior is the most important decision you'll ever make! Nothing comes close to this decision; not your career and surely not your wife. It will change your life now and your eternal destiny. There is no decision that could be made that is like it. It would be very sad for me to teach you that Jesus was and is God and not give you an opportunity to repent and to receive Him into your heart as your God and Savior. Will you accept Him as God and not just another good man like some believe and say?

God has promised, "If thou shalt confess with thy mouth the Lord Jesus, and shalt believe in thine heart that God hath raised him from the dead, thou shalt be saved. For with the heart man believeth unto righteousness; and with the mouth confession is made unto salvation…. For whosoever shall call upon the name of the Lord shall be saved" (Romans 10:9-10, 13).

By His grace, God has already done everything and His part to provide for your salvation. Your part is simply to believe and receive. It is the easiest decision. This is a heart decision, not a head decision. Now is the acceptable time, today is the day of salvation (2 Corinthians 6:2). Why wait?

Pray this prayer and mean it sincerely from your heart:

Jesus,

I confess that You are my Lord and Savior. I believe in my heart that God raised You from the dead. By faith in Your Word, I receive salvation, now. Thank You for saving me!

The very moment you commit your life to Jesus Christ, the truth of His Word instantly comes to pass in your spirit. Now that you're born again, you are brand new on the inside of you. God has created in you a new spirit and a new heart.

Receive the Baptism of the Holy Spirit

Living a Christian life is not just a difficult thing to do but an impossible thing. You need help. So, because it is impossible to live a victorious, Christian life without the baptism of the Holy Spirit, the Lord wants to give you the supernatural power you need to live this new life. We receive power when we receive the baptism of the Holy Spirit (Acts 1:8).

It's as simple as asking and receiving. When we ask for the Holy Spirit, the Lord will give Him to us (Luke 11:10, 13). All you have to do is ask, believe, and receive!

Pray:

Father,

I recognize my need for Your power to live this new life. Please fill me with Your Holy Spirit. By faith, I receive Him right now! Thank You for baptizing me. Holy Spirit, You are welcome in my life.

Congratulations! Now you're filled with God's super-natural power. Some syllables from a language you don't recognize will rise up from your heart to your mouth (See 1 Corinthians 14:14). Go ahead and speak those syllables. As you speak them out loud by faith, you're releasing God's power from within and building yourself up in the Spirit (See 1 Corinthians 14:4). You can do this whenever and wherever you like.

It doesn't really matter whether you felt anything or not when you prayed to receive the Lord and His Spirit. If you believed in your heart that you received, then God's Word promises that you received. "Therefore I say unto you, What things soever ye desire, when ye pray, believe that ye receive them, and ye shall have them" (Mark 11:24). God always honors His Word — believe it!

About the Author

Rich Kanyali was born in Kampala, Uganda, on June 2, 1987. He lived there until after high school when he received Christ into his heart. In Uganda, it's not automatic that most people go on to university, but God opened a door for Rich to go to India and pursue a Bachelor of Commerce (BCOM) at Garden City College in Bangalore, an affiliate of Bangalore University. After his graduation in 2010, he moved to the United States to pursue his MBA. However, financially, things fell apart, and he could not afford school as an international student. God spoke to him to go to Charis Bible College and prepare for the ministry that God had called him to.

He graduated in 2017 with a Masters in Biblical Studies (MBS) and a license to preach the gospel of Jesus Christ. He has been teaching and bringing godly insight to the scriptures since 2008 when he was in India. He established his first Bible study group with a few students at Garden City College. The group grew, and he later turned it over to another leader, whom he had raised up. He has been establishing groups and teaching God's Word to whomever will listen!

He was also an ordained teacher and leader at his local church in India, tasked with leading and teaching the Adult Sunday School. He is an author, a seasoned student of the Word, and a teacher by gifting and calling. Rich's passion is to teach God's Word to the body of Christ with a greater emphasis on grace, faith, and making disciples, which in return will quickly turn the world right side up for King Jesus! He is also the author of his book, ***Jesus; God or Man?***

He is married to his lovely wife Joanna, and they have a beautiful daughter named Shalom.

CPSIA information can be obtained
at www.ICGtesting.com
Printed in the USA
FFOW03n0428130418
46230347-47580FF